OH, MY MIND

YOU ARE LIKE A SMALL CHILD

notionpress.com

OH, MY MIND

YOU ARE LIKE A SMALL CHILD

Empowerment Series by

GAURAV DHAMEJAA

notionpress.com

Notion Press

Old No. 38, New No. 6

McNichols Road, Chetpet

Chennai - 600 031

First Published by Notion Press 2016

ISBN 978-93-5206-648-3

CONTENTS

FOREWORD

In this handy pocketbook, which is brimming with power punches and spiritual information, Gaurav has given simplified Yogic techniques for guiding the mind towards the right path. An untrained mind makes one create the situations that one actually wants to avoid in life. This is because the mind is like a child who attempts to repeat the same act that he or she is restricted from doing. So, rather than focusing on what one fears and what one wishes to avoid in life, one needs to discipline the mind to focus on what one wishes to do or have in life. Gaurav speaks about the path to surrendering to the truth or higher self rather than being a slave of one's emotions and stored memories.

As stated in the Yoga Sutras of Patanjali, "yoga chitta vritti nirodha," which translates to "Yoga is the silencing of the definitions of the mind." In this book, Gaurav has provided very easy, doable methods for achieving this through achar (right behaviour), vichar (right intention), ahar (healthy diet) and vihar (right activities). These pave the way for training the mind, body and senses. He speaks about the dos and don'ts related to personal habits and behaviour. There is a difference between the principles of behaviour that are acceptable to society as a whole and the rules of individual behaviour.

The inculcation of steadfastness, faith, compassion, honesty and absence of greed are what help one achieve self-discipline. Gaurav emphasizes purity of body, mind and speech, peace accompanied by contentment, devotion, forgiveness, self-acceptance, svadhyaya or self-study and divine surrender. These would help one attain super-consciousness. The book has simple tips on Asanas and Pranayam that one could follow in daily life as well as handy affirmations.

Ultimately, he says that it is detachment from role play that helps a person accept the change and flow that are a part of life.

Ms Neeta Singhal

Founder: Rudraksha Ratna and Chakrayog

ACKNOWLEDGMENTS

I am grateful to my Heavenly father and mother, my Satguru: Guruji Maharaj; my masters: Mahavtaar Babaji, Lahri Mahasaya ji, Sri Yukteshwar ji, Parmahansa Yoganandi ji, Swami Kriyananda, Swami Rama and Yogiraj Gurunath Sidhnath; my teachers: Dr Brian Weiss, Mr Yuvraj Kapadia, Madam Dharmadevi, Ms Neeta Singhal and everyone who acted as my teacher either knowingly or unknowingly in various adverse situations and helped me choose the correct path.

I am immensely grateful to my parents and family, especially my wife, for her unflinching support in all my endeavours; my clients, for helping me learn through their experiences, which otherwise would not have been possible and my friends and relatives, for always believing in me.

Special thanks to Sheeshir Singh for giving apt shape to the content of this book.

INTRODUCTION

The mind is like a small child – extremely divine yet vulnerable to wrongness! Whenever we restrict a child from doing something, he or she would do exactly that thing. This is definitely an ignorant passive-aggressive behaviour. Similarly, when we try to restrict our mind from doing something, we cause great trouble to ourselves and eventually end up doing the same thing. But this does not mean that we should keep on doing all the things that we are not supposed to do. Discipline is very important, and right discipline enables one to enjoy real freedom. Discipline and freedom go hand in hand. The basic principle to be followed while training and disciplining the mind is by becoming its friend and then doing all those things that we should do for leading a better life.

For example, we plan to go on a diet and choose to avoid eating fatty food by training our mind with the thought of not eating that food, then sooner or later we will end up eating the same food. On the other hand, if we become friends with our mind and train it regularly with the thought of eating simple food, which is the exact opposite of fatty food, then we shall definitely find great success!

Likewise, we must train our mind with the things we want in life and not with those that are not needed by us. There is a general tendency to say things which we don't want, like "I don't want tension in life," "I don't want any non-sense in my life" etc. Rather, if we consciously train our mind with "I want peace in my life," "I want a meaningful life," then we shall observe desired changes happening around us within sometime.

When exposed to stressful situations, the mind stores our reaction and response to those situations. Such reactions become reference points for the mind when we are again exposed to similar situations. It is at such times that our responses are tested. If we do not train the mind with the ability to give positive and balanced responses, we will be subject to slavery of already stored negative reactions and will feel and behave in the same way.

This book provides tips on training and nourishing our mind to avoid such slavery.

1

PRACTISE SIMPLICITY

Unknowingly, we allow our energy to be wasted on useless things, which eventually make our lives meaningless. We suffer because of an unintentional negative training of mind, which works on an autonomous mode with respect to the training it has! Gossiping, impulsive reactions, hatred, jealousy, over-attachment, fault finding, lying, overeating, seeking happiness only in big things, being judgmental, egoism, egotism, anger, lust, over-expectation, blaming, cribbing, excessive questioning, fearfulness, nervousness, restlessness, cravings, addictions, irritation, painfulness, helplessness and so on are some of the unwholesome psychological traits with which the mind is usually trained. A tremendous amount of functional energy is drained out because of such traits.

Also, today's modern world offers a highly unnatural environment that is experienced by our senses. Long exposures to high-resolution display screens, high decibels that are created by sound effects, mobile telephonic conversations, excessive use of processed food and so on consume a lot of our functional energy. These serve as one of the main reasons of stress!

What Should You Do?

Train your mind with the essence of "simplicity!" Practising simplicity is the answer to all the negative traits, and it is the best way to conserve functional energy.

Smile

One of the greatest spiritual masters of India, Parmahansa Yoganandaji said, "Be a smile millionaire!" Many relationships suffer from savourlessness, because the people involved in those relationships do not smile. When we smile and allow our heart, which has all the divine love, to smile through our facial muscles, a strong vibration of love fills the surroundings and one feels a sense of harmony. A smile aids in closing many negative files that are opened in our subconsciousness. Our soul knows all our past relationships, and that is why sometimes we naturally feel attracted towards a few people whom we do not even know. To such strangers, we offer an unsaid and unnoticed but natural smile filled with divine love and thus, we feel wonderful about ourselves. This is the proof that a smile is a measuring gauge of our love for both ourselves and others. If we consciously practise smiling and train our mind to offer a smile of humility to everyone, we shall avoid innumerable arguments and save a great amount of our functional energy, which would enable us to lead a utilitarian life!

"Be a smile millionaire!"

Close Your Ears

Most people experience that a particular song or tune goes on repeating itself in the subconsciousness despite their being passive to the sound and not hearing it actively. This proves that our ears are always exposed to environmental noise, and the same impressions are fed into our subconscious mind. The life force directed outwards through the sense of hearing is tremendously wasted, as the ears are always open. Also, the malefic practices of exposing ourselves to very high decibel music and staying away from the natural music of nature and the sound of silence in the universe cause a great deal of loss of mental peace. If we practise the closing of the ears with our thumbs for at least five minutes in a day, we will be able to conserve a lot of energy.

Eat Right

> Never eat while watching television. It leads to overeating.

Food can be a blessing if properly understood. However, it can become a curse if we abuse it or become its slave! We eat to feed our body with the vital nutrients that are required for its proper functioning. EAT means "energy and taste." Eating right food includes a balance of fruits, vegetables, cereals, pulses, nuts and seeds. The digestive system consumes a lot of energy, because we ignore it. It is extremely important to eat your meal in a quiet place with your full attention only on your food. Never eat while watching television. It leads to overeating.

Meal servings should be short, and one should adapt the habit of eating every two hours. It is also a necessity to chew the food that we eat to a level where it becomes almost in liquid form; this would enable us to get the maximum energy and taste out of it. Gulping of food leads to the consumption of exorbitant energy during digestion. Eating right saves tremendous energy!

Notice Your Breath

The biggest of all truths is the current time: this very moment in which you are consciously reading but also breathing involuntarily. If we start focusing on our breath on a regular basis, we will be more in touch with the feeling of the present and closer to the truth of life! This will also help in relaxing our body and mind and will improve our overall efficiency.

Feel Great

We are an integral part of this inconceivably vast creation around us. We are here to play a role in this live drama of the cosmos and to make the drama more interesting and meaningful. Realization of this privilege is sufficient to feel great about ourselves.

Exercise 1

Sit upright with a straight spine, close your eyes, close your ears with your thumbs, focus on your breath and smile. When you open your eyes after sometime, you will feel great about yourself!

2

STRIKE A BALANCE

Things that we like the most are easy to do! But the things that are important for our overall growth as an individual and as an integral part of this world are difficult to do. This is a general perception of the mind! Becoming conscious of the things that we should do and devoting time and energy to such things will create a wonderful balance in our lives.

Filling up Voids

An empty space between a desire in us and our ground reality is called a "void." Practically speaking, each one of us has voids. Ignorantly, we try to fill such voids with malefic practices of regret, rejection and resentment. However, voids can only be filled with conscious and balanced practices of *love, acceptance and forgiveness!*

We Can Give Only What We Have

A great deal of imbalance is caused in our lives while offering something to others that we do not have for ourselves. We must love ourselves if we want to give love to others. To accept others, we must accept ourselves and to forgive others, we must truly forgive ourselves. This is an ongoing process!

Accepting Our Present Condition

Acceptance improves attention and attention begets an opportunity to climb the next step towards our desire with safety, security and stability.

If we climb upstairs with our attention focused only on the door we have to reach, we might tumble downstairs. Likewise, if our attention is only on the desire and not on the present situation we are in, we might never see our desires getting fulfilled! Acceptance of the present condition is the first step towards the journey of success in any aspect of life!

Acceptance improves attention and attention begets an opportunity to climb the next step towards our desire with safety, security and stability.

Exercise 2

Sit upright with a straight spine, close your eyes, place the palms of both your hands on your chest, focus on your breath, smile and loudly affirm, "I love and accept myself and sincerely forgive myself."

3

PRACTISE HAPPINESS

Happiness is a combination of satisfaction and peace! We draw satisfaction from the outside world. Whenever we achieve something or any of our desires is fulfilled, we feel satisfied. It is that state when other desires have no importance at that point of time. But the moment our attention is drawn towards something that is unfulfilled, we again become dissatisfied. That is why happiness is incomplete in spite of all the materialistic achievements. We must understand that even the richest man on earth can never claim that he is the happiest man on earth.

Happiness can only be complete if a feeling of peace is experienced along with the feeling of satisfaction.

When at any moment of our life fears, insecurity, anxiety, inconsistency, instability, lethargy, anger, sadness, frustration, irritation and so on have no place, the feeling that is experienced can be easily called "peace."

Happiness can only be complete if a feeling of peace is experienced along with the feeling of satisfaction.

Peace is an ocean of joy within us and is not dependent on the outside world being in our favour. Unlike peace, satisfaction is drawn only from the outside world when it acts according to what we feel is right. If we work more on peace and go outside to seek satisfaction with the feelings of peace and joy, we would be extremely happy.

Enjoy

Enjoyment must be understood as "an enhanced feeling of joy". When we feel that joy within us and then go outside seeking the fun of the world, only then can we truly enjoy ourselves. Otherwise, it is just another formality in life!

Be Cheerful

This is a great outward expression of true happiness. When we dance without inhibition and dance for ourselves and not to gain the attention of others; when we sing and become one with the music, forgetting the notes and when we write something, becoming one with the feelings, we will shed all the reasons to feel gloomy and experience true happiness!

Exercise 3

Sit upright with a straight spine, close your eyes, place both your palms on your chest, take three deep breaths, smile and loudly affirm, "I dive into the ocean of peace and enjoy my life to the fullest."

4

PRACTISE CONTINUANCE

In infinity lies the glory of the Creator! Nothing in the world is permanent, except change. So, when everything is infinite, ever changing and never ending, it means that our efforts towards achieving success in every aspect must also continue. Materialistic achievement gives a glimpse of the need to be consistent in our efforts. We have to make efforts till the time we do not achieve. When we achieve something, we have to make efforts to sustain and maintain it! Practising continuance is, therefore, mandatory in this journey from the finite to the infinite!

Walking on the Right Path

There is always a way for everyone to reach one's desires. The first and foremost thing is to properly understand the desire itself and also to know whether it is worth spending energy on finding the right path to fulfil the same. If the desire is strong and becomes a "will," one can attract the right path to fulfil that desire. Once a path is defined, consistently walking on it without getting distracted will take us to our destination!

Practise Patience

Being calm and focused begets patience.

The implementation of patience in any aspect of life requires understanding, courage and strength. Patience is that powerful tool that has the ability to change the environment around us. It is the most active thing to do and can only be achieved when we consistently work on handling our own emotions rather than on always trying to control our surroundings. When we regularly work on improving our emotional response to a given situation, we put an end to impulsive reactions and become like a magnet that attracts positivity and dispels negativity.

Being calm and focused begets patience.

Understanding Success

Success is an ongoing journey! Being successful is a perception of mind, which, if properly understood, can act as a catalyst in converting seeds into fruits every time. There is nothing as such that can be called a failure! It is so, because every time when the result is not as per the requirement, it means to say that either we need to understand the same way in a better manner or we just need to try some other way in which things will work. Success is completely in one's mind, and it should not be misunderstood with the possession of materialistic assets.

Success is that potential strength that enables things to work in our favour!

Exercise 4

Sit upright with a straight spine, close your eyes, place both your palms on your chest, take three deep breaths, smile and loudly affirm, "I patiently keep walking on the path of success."

5

DEVELOP FAITH

Faith is the biggest strength of a human being! It is that power that helps us feel that we are supported, guided and protected at all times.

We must understand that there is an unseen hand behind the working of this universe. An infinite intelligence and power allows the earth and all the other planets of the solar system to move on their orbits and not run into each other! We must consider why the ocean does not run into the sky or why we walk on the grass and the grass does not walk on us!

We tend to concentrate on finite things and finite understandings and forget that we actually belong to the infinite. We must realize that we are the creation of a magnanimous Creator, whose ever-watching eyes are watching every action of ours, who knows every thought of ours and who is always present both within and around us to provide us with everything we need! He lives in the feeling of faith within us.

Faith is the result of an amalgamation of surrender, devotion and perception.

Faith is the result of an amalgamation of surrender, devotion and perception.

Divine Surrender

This is the bravest thing to do! If we consider any job is out of our capacity, we must remind ourselves that the owner of the universe can do the same thing with simplicity, grace and ease. This curbs egoism and when we consciously make Him the doer of all things and give all our weaknesses and difficulties to Him, all our fears will fly away from us. When we start living life without unnecessary fears, we truly open up ourselves to His unconditional love. It is that feeling of His Love that gives birth to devotion in us for Him.

Devotion

Devotion, the precursor of perception, enables us to be in touch with our true selves. The power of devotion makes our heart both a giver and a receiver of unconditional love, and the purity of our soul is reflected by our heart. Then, all human beings are one for us and we become unbiased and unconditional in our approach.

Devotion is developed by praying to our Heavenly Father and Mother as a child would. One should pray intensely and unceasingly, for instance, talking to God all the time with great belief that He is listening to everything and that He will answer all our prayers in some form or the other. Devotion is only possible if it is unconditional in every way! If we pray and expect immediate results, that is not devotion.

Remember, devotion is felt only after surrender, which, in itself, is a mark of freeing ourselves from the results of our actions as we give ourselves to our Heavenly Father to take care of us in the way that He wants to!

Perception

We all are blessed with a strong sense of knowingness. All our thoughts, answers and resolutions are already present within us.

To reach that point, we need to merge our consciousness into the subconsciousness. Then, with complete surrender and devotion, we should enter deep into a zone that is beyond the subconscious. This zone is known as super-consciousness! This is where the "library of ether" is stored within us! It is that state in which reason meets intelligence and both of them become united. That is the state of "being in the now!"

The depth of perception may vary for every individual, but it is available to everyone. The greatest thing to perceive is the way through which we can become one with our highest self, who is the all knower, always in joy, who feels absolutely safe and secure all the time, who rises above all situations and who has the capacity to weigh both the pros and cons and choose the best in a given situation. That is our real strength. That is real freedom!

Exercise 5

Sit upright with a straight spine, close your eyes, focus on your breath, place your hands in the prayer position, smile and loudly affirm "I surrender myself to the infinite and receive intelligence in my life."

6

BREAK THE RULES BUT FOLLOW THE PRINCIPLES

Discipline means practising the basic principles regularly. If we know the principles well, rules are not important. "Rules restrict whereas principles enhance." For example, we all know that exercise is important for our body. So, exercising daily is the basic principle. If we start thinking that exercise only in the morning is beneficial and make it a rule, we might forget the actual principle because of this self-created rule. The basic principle is that the best time to do anything in life is when you feel inspired to do it and when you do it!

If life is a journey from ignorance to awareness, principally, we all are travellers carrying our own backpack of experiences. To realize the real purpose of our existence, we must move on the path of life despite bad patches. No matter what happens to us, time moves on and life goes on. This is the basic principle of life.

"Rules restrict whereas principles enhance."

Anything that happens to us or to the people around us places us in a virtual classroom of learning. What we learn decides our future. Anything learnt, consciously or subconsciously, can be best called an "experience." People weigh an experience to be either good (positive) or bad (negative). It is a very tricky situation when whatever we experience becomes a driving force for us, thus making us either an achiever or a loser in our life.

Scientists discovered that a human mind thinks nearly 60,000 thoughts in one day. Now, whether we are conscious of it or not, every thought generates an emotion in our subconsciousness. Regardless of whichever way one considers this, it is nothing but energy in motion, which we call an "emotion." It is this emotion that is responsible for what we are and what we will be in future.

The whole of creation is based on laws and their respective operating principles. As one's consciousness expands, these laws become more and more apparent and evident in one's life. To give you a small example, whenever I get angry or frustrated in a situation and I do not train my mind with the opposite emotion, I keep on attracting more frustrating situations that make me angrier. This happened to me many times and finally I decided to change my response to frustrating situations. To my surprise, I experienced that those frustrating situations were resolved on their own. Initially, I used to feel that some miracles have started happening in my life, but as my awareness increased, I realized that there are some laws operating behind such resolution. I eventually started relating every situation to some law and started understanding the same. Some of the basic laws that I perceived are given next:

Law of Linearity

Time moves in a linear way. This highlights the concept of past, present and future. Out of these three parameters of time, we can only control our present. So, by applying this basic principle of concentrating only on our present and making an effort to improve it, we can resolve a lot of our problems.

Law of Duality

The opposite of everything exists simultaneously. There are many practical examples in our daily lives that indicate that this law is very obvious: To start with, we have pleasure–pain, peace–hate, day–night, success–failure, good–bad, loyalty–betrayal, material–spiritual and so on. My understanding says that if I am experiencing a disturbing emotion, then as per this law, an exactly opposite emotion also exists for me simultaneously. So principally, if I remind myself of that opposite emotion, I am creating an opportunity for myself to experience it soon.

Law of Rationality

At any point of time, we have to make a choice, consciously or subconsciously, to take our life forward! But there is a constant demand of making more conscious choices to learn and experience this show of life in a better way. So, the law of rationality teaches us to have an aerial view of situations, understand the pros and cons and finally make a conscious and practical choice for overall betterment.

Law of Love and Acceptance

Love is the ultimate consciousness existing in this universe. The vibrational rhythm originating from the feeling of love has that divine energy that is required to change any reality that is not liked or admired by us. The whole universe emanates unconditional love, and we are also made out of the same consciousness. If we understand this fact and accept it the way it is, we will give birth to an unbiased feeling of care, nourishment and divine intention within us. So, the demand of this law of love and acceptance is that we must love and accept ourselves and hence love and accept others!

Law of Forgiveness

Undesirable and bad things that happened to us in the past sometimes have such a strong influence on us that it becomes difficult for us to forget them. Hence, we suffer the ill effects caused by the feelings of regret, rejection and resentment. The only way to forget is to forgive. So, the law of forgiveness demands that we forgive ourselves for everything that we could not do in the past and forgive others for everything that they did to us.

Law of Surrender

Everything in this universe is expressing something to us in various forms. When we keep our eyes and ears open to a given situation, we become aware of that situation.

Awareness is the first step towards resolution, as it begets many options in life from which we could choose. A choice made out of awareness and understanding gives good results in life.

So, the law of surrender demands us to be good listeners, become aware, understand and then make a choice.

Law of Attraction

We are like magnets having a magnetic field around us flowing from head to toe. It is through the strength of this magnetic field that we attract good or bad things in our lives. When we desire something and run after it, the same thing starts running away from us. Likewise, when we want to get rid of something and try very hard to run away or escape from it, the same thing follows us more strongly. Such situations arise when we develop a tendency of becoming either overexcited or deeply sad. Such emotions cause a dent in our magnetic field and weaken it tremendously.

So the law of attraction demands us to be more centered, focused and balanced in our approach in order to attract things desired by us and to dispel those that are not needed!

Law of Loyalty

The feeling of loyalty originates from the sense of oneness. It can be practised between two individuals or among a group of people or even with an idea or a thought. We are completely deluded by the nature of life on earth, which beholds duality. Such delusion separates us from each other and makes us suffer the ill effects of feelings of being incomplete and lonely.

Great masters call loyalty "the first law of life." It is so, because it reminds us of our expansive nature when it comes to being honest to our commitments. It makes us closer to the truth of the existence of this universe, that is, oneness.

So, the law of loyalty demands us to be true to ourselves in relationships and commitments by becoming one with a person or a thought.

7

NONATTACHED ATTITUDE

In this world of duality, we are utterly deceived when we seek happiness in worldly pleasures. By nature, pleasure hides pain behind itself. It is our ignorance to attach ourselves to worldly things and achievements. By saying so, I do not mean that we should not involve ourselves in worldly activities. Even God is actively engaged in this show but with a non-attached attitude.

To understand this, it would be good to think of your favourite actor. He must have acted in many movies and performed various roles. In some movie, he might have been a rich guy; whereas in another, he might have been a poor guy. In some role, he might have been a lover but in another, he might have been a rebel. Likewise, he might have performed many contrasting roles. Now, think of this actor as an individual. In real life, he might be a very different person than the roles he had played in movies. When performing his role, the actor knows that he is playing a character. To give his best performance, he has to feel the character intensely. But when his performance is over, he has to come back to his normal self. This is a classic example of engagement in an activity with a nonattached attitude.

Our mind has a tendency to look for alike emotions. If we are too attached to our roles, this attachment causes fears and insecurities and can make us behave either dangerously dynamic or extremely static. Mostly, people fear loss of money, position, power, reputation, status, relationships, love, loved ones, health, wealth and happiness. These fears cause some prominent symptoms such as anxiety, nervousness, panic, frightfulness and helplessness.

If we train our mind with the idea that this world is nothing but a show of good and evil, light and shadow, responsibility and reciprocity and we are here in this physical body as a character to play a certain role of a father, mother, sister, brother, son, daughter, serviceman, businessman, entrepreneur, sportsperson, social activist, painter, singer, writer, doctor, healer, spiritual guide and so on, we will perform our roles well and also with a nonattached attitude.

This will free us from a very strong and vicious circle of pain and pleasure that emerges from attachment.

With this understanding a question might arise in your mind that the actor knows when his performance is over and then he comes back to his normal self. But how do we know about it in our real life? Is it when death comes, then we are free from the role?

The answer is simple. Just think what happens to our role when we sleep. In sleep, we completely detach ourselves from all situations of life and become unconscious of our character as well. We lose bodily consciousness and are close to our soul consciousness, which is all knowing and is always in peace. That is a glimpse of our normal self! But when we wake up, our role starts again and we have to perform this role again. I know you must be thinking that sleeping is the best answer for taking a break from our role. Sleep certainly helps, but it is a temporary relief. In sleep, awareness is lost! This means that we again become ignorant. Ignorance can never lead us to the truth of life, but only awareness will. You might now be thinking that if sleep is not the real answer, then what is it? The answer is meditation.

So, What Is Meditation?

8

MEDITATION

All over the world, most people do not understand meditation only because they are unsure about the concept of meditation. Meditation is a state of expanded awareness, and it is the first step towards the resolution of all problems in life. It is such a wonderful state in which healing happens at all levels of our existence.

However, it is like telling somebody how sugar tastes. One cannot explain this in words but can surely make the other person experience it by making him or her taste sugar. Likewise, words are inadequate to describe meditation, but I can certainly provide you a few steps, which, if you practise regularly, will lead you to experience the state of meditation!

1. Invocation: Acknowledging the "Parent Source"

Who created your body, mind, senses and soul? If you do not know the answer, then it is not a bad idea to ask your parents. May be, they have an answer!

In my experience, all parents acknowledge that apart from the act that they performed for their child's conception in the mother's womb and taking care of the needs of the foetus through the mother's diet and routine, they have no active participation in making the baby. So, someone created the baby's body, mind and senses! Can doctors create a human body or mind? Till date, the answer is "no." But someone created all of us. There is a creator behind our human existence. I call that creator the real "parent source."

So, invocation is all about inviting that parent source, who created us, to witness every act, thought and intention of ours so that we feel supported, guided and protected in every moment we live. Invocation gives a strong message to the cells of the body, to every corner of the mind and to the senses and soul consciousness that we are serious about taking charge of our life.

Invocation to Practice

Heavenly Father and Mother, bless this moment of my life for my immediate and highest good, for my loved ones, my family, society, nation, world, humanity on earth and this universe.

2. Conscious Breathing: Take Charge of Your Life Force

Without food and water, it is still possible to survive for a few days. But without breath, it is difficult to survive for even a few minutes. We all are breathing every moment. Breathing is such an important activity and we are not even conscious of it. It is high time for you to become aware of your breath now! Given next are a few techniques that must be practised daily, to keep the flow of life force smooth and easy:

Sit comfortably but with a straight spine. If need be, place a cushion below your hips to support your spine. This would enable you to be straight for a longer period.

a. Inhale through the nose and exhale through the mouth

Consciously inhale a deep breath through your nose. Hold your breath to the count of three and exhale through your mouth as if you are blowing off a candle. Practise this five to ten times, twice daily.

b. Alternate nostril breathing

Close your right nostril with your right thumb. Inhale deeply through your left nostril. Now, with the index finger of your right hand, close your left nostril as well. Loosen your right thumb on your right nostril and exhale slowly from your right nostril.

In the same position, now inhale deeply from your right nostril. After taking a deep breath, close your right nostril with your right thumb. Now, loosen your right hand index finger from your left nostril and exhale slowly from your left nostril.

The process just mentioned is one cycle. Practise ten cycles, twice daily.

c. Energy bouncing – visualize feet to head and head to feet breath

Inhale deeply: While inhaling, visualize that a cold current of energy is rising up from your feet to your head. Hold your breath to the count of three. Now, exhale slowly. While exhaling, visualize that a warm current of energy is climbing down from your head to your feet.

The process just mentioned is one cycle. Practise ten cycles, twice daily.

3. Guiding Attention

Energy follows attention. This is a universal fact. Wherever your attention is, your energy follows it. Many people experience absentmindedness. Such people, unknowingly, waste their functional energy on those emotions that they are not even aware of.

In my healing practice, I always use one modality with all my clients for achieving the best results and that modality is "Become aware of your emotions." Bring your awareness and attention to "how you feel." This is the most important step towards the resolution of problems in life.

For example, if you have a habit of getting irritated and shouting at people even for small things of practically no importance, then just sit down and ask yourself the following:

i. How do I feel when I get irritated and shout?
ii. What happens next after I have done this?
iii. On a scale of 0 to 10, how much willing I am to change this habit of mine?

Note down your answers.

Now, make the first answer as the point of attention for your mind. Supposedly, your answer is "I feel bad." Imagine this feeling of "bad" is in front of you. Inhale through the nose and forcefully exhale through the mouth, as if you are throwing this feeling out of your body, mind, senses, soul and surroundings. Do it till the time you really feel you have thrown it out of your system.

Repeat the same for your second answer also. Then, simply smile and keep all your attention only and only on your smile.

Guiding your attention can help you in releasing various rigid, stubborn, heavy and downward emotions and can make you feel much relieved, relaxed, nonattached and free!

4. Practising Concentration

When the mind is clear from useless and disturbing emotions, only then can one really concentrate. Concentration means bringing the subject of the mind to be focused on one point of the object.

To choose the point of the object, a few options are given next, which I find to be extremely useful:

a. **A candle flame**: Place a candle at eye level and at your arm's length distance. Light it and begin to observe the tip of its flame. Simply follow the tip wherever it goes. No matter what distracts you, just keep on reminding yourself "I have to focus only on the tip of the flame." This technique is known as "Tratak (steady gazing)."

b. **A specific mantra**: I believe in the tremendous power of mantras. These are sound frequencies having very potent vibrations that are capable of cleansing and balancing our spiritual anatomy. You can choose to simply chant "AUM" to start with till the time you become more aware of other mantras. The important part of chanting a mantra is to maintain your attention first at the point between the eyebrows and then chant. This gives great results.

c. **Choose an affirmation**: Choose a specific affirmation with which you completely resonate in this phase of your life. Again, focus on the point between the eyebrows and then chant your affirmation.

The following affirmation from my side is given next:

"I keep moving with faith, courage and patience."

9

ANATOMY BEYOND PHYSICAL BODY

Thanks to the instrumentality of conventional medical science, today's human beings are sufficiently aware of their physical anatomy. Many preventive tests and early diagnosis of a disease or disorder help in resolving various issues of the physical body to a large extent.

But many of my clients who have been suffering from diabetes, cancer, depression, psychiatric problems, autoimmune conditions, Parkinson's disease and other neurological issues and the like did not know anything about why such diseases happen. All they knew was that they had to deal with them by using medicines and adopting some lifestyle changes. Honestly speaking, medicine management helps to a great extent, but it is not the complete answer to such chronic issues. This is because of the fact that even today's medical science genuinely does not know the root cause of these chronic diseases or disorders. It took quite some time for us to realize that it is not only food that is solely responsible for heart problems but also hypertension and lack of sleep are major reasons. From there comes the concept of stress management, leading to the deflation of hypertension to have a healthy heart, healthy living and better efficiency.

Nothing happens without a reason! If this is true, then chronic conditions such as diabetes, cancer, depression, autoimmune conditions and so on also have their root causes. Diagnosis that is limited to hereditary or childhood issues is actually a limited understanding of this subject. We now need to understand something beyond our physical anatomy!

We have been conditioned with a limiting belief that we are only this physical body. When this body dies, we die and the show is over. I am not going to digress from this subject to life and death, but just for the sake of understanding, I am using these words.

Nowadays, many doctors also realize that most of our physical and circumstantial issues are psychosomatic. In simple understanding, most of the problems in some or the other form start first in the mind.

My intention is to take you further. We are unique, because we have been made with unique components of existence. We are made of five bodies, three minds, six senses (Sense of Sight, Smell, Taste, Touch, Hearing and Knowingness) and an engaged and witnessing soul consciousness!

Sounds complicated? Not yet...

Furthermore, we have 72,000 astral tubes, 108 marma points and 7 main energy distribution centres called "Chakras." The sum total of everything is known as "Aura."

This completes our real anatomy. I call it "spiritual anatomy."

Now, we must understand that the root cause of any issue can come from any part of our spiritual anatomy. We work with medicines to combat the symptoms of our physical and mental issues. Likewise, we can work with some techniques to combat the root cause of our problems coming from any part of our spiritual anatomy.

This brings us to the concept of yoga and the Yogic way of living.

10

YOGIC WAY OF LIVING

The intention behind writing this book is to offer simple viewpoints about whatever comes to the awareness of one's mind. So, I am not going to get into the technicalities of Yogic principles and Sutras, but would rather offer a very simple understanding for everyone to absorb and implement in their lives.

Yoga, in my perception and experience, simply means "integration."

- Integration of body with mind
- Integration of body and mind with senses
- Integration of body, mind and senses with breath
- Integration of body, mind, senses and breath with life force energy (individual Prana)
- Integration of body, mind, senses, breath and individual Prana with cosmic life force energy (universal Prana or Kundalini Shakti)

No matter how flavourful a dish is, if it lacks salt, there will be no taste.

Likewise, integration is fruitful only when awareness is added to the components of body, mind, senses, breath and Prana.

Thus, Yoga Means "Integration with Awareness."

Visualize your favourite dancer dancing to one of your favourite songs! Just observe the integration of his or her body, mind, and sense of hearing, breath, energy and awareness, which enables him or her to move any part of his or her body in sync with the music. This is a practical example of understanding the real essence of yoga. This essence can be used by us for anything and everything we need and desire in our life.

We have two aspects of our living. One is the materialistic aspect, and the other is our spiritual aspect. Unless one is satisfied with their material aspect, they will not evolve spiritually with ease. Likewise, if one pays attention only to their spiritual aspect, they will be off grounded, away from ground reality and will experience material instability.

There is an utmost need to create a balance between these two aspects. Given next is my understanding about how to maintain this balance by practising the basic essence of yoga, that is, integration with awareness.

Material Aspect

Bring the index finger of your right hand on your sternum (point where the rib cage meets). Place the index finger of your left hand at the base of your spine, where your tail bone ends. Now, become aware of the area between these two fingers. Within this area there are three most important energy distribution centres called "Chakras": Root Centre (Mooladhar Chakra) at the base of the spine near to where your finger is; Sacral Centre (Swadisthana Chakra) just above your sexual organs and Solar Plexus (Manipura Chakra) at your Navel Centre. These are the Chakras responsible for material growth. They deal with career and financial stability, success, power, free will to make a choice, satisfaction, challenging attitude, seeking enjoyment in material achievements and so on.

Now, become aware of the organs present in this area. You have your stomach, spleen, liver, gall bladder, pancreas, intestines, kidneys, some important glands, sexual organs and excretory organs. If you have any physical health issue related to these organs, such as diabetes, indigestion, liver problems, kidney or gall bladder stones, constipation, piles, prostrate problem, polycystic ovarian disease (PCOD), infertility, knee pain, leg pain, osteoarthritis, blood and related disorders, cancer cell growth and so on, it means to say that your Chakras for this area are not functioning properly and they are either blocked or imbalanced.

Now, why are the Chakras blocked or imbalanced? Within these Chakras there is the flow of Prana. It gets blocked, because the mind, which is intricately woven within this area, carries heavy and downward emotions and feelings of not being supported, self-doubt, helplessness, powerlessness, indecisiveness, irrationality, impatience and frustration and also other similar emotions or feelings. Such emotions attract similar emotions and then make an emotional chain. Such an emotional chain attracts similar emotional chains and then make it a belief. Once a belief is made, it starts storing a lot of Prana to sustain itself. This causes Prana deficiency in that area.

You can now imagine how important it is to supplement this area with Prana.

The best way to supplement yourself with Prana is to move your breath up and down within that area with a very strong intention and complete awareness. Expand your awareness and start reaching out to every part of that area. You can do this while walking and jogging; practicing asanas or other related exercises that energize this area. Whatever you do, do it with a strong will and complete awareness. That is the key to a Yogic way of living.

Spiritual Aspect

Bring the index finger of your right hand on to the top of your head. Place the index finger of your left hand at the centre of your chest. Now, become aware of the area between these two fingers. There are four main Chakras in this area: Heart Centre (Anahat Chakra), exactly where your left hand index finger is, Throat Centre (Vishudha Chakra) at the U cavity where your neck ends, Third Eye Centre (Ajna/Aagya Chakra) at the point between the eyebrows and Crown Centre (Sahasrara Chakra) at the top of your head where your right hand index finger is placed.

These Chakras are responsible for spiritual growth. They deal with love, acceptance, forgiveness, power of expression, aerial view of situations, contentment, giving attitude, divine reciprocity, intention to help without selfish motives, higher learnings from Vedic scriptures, devotion towards one's guru and so on.

Next, become aware of the organs present in this area. You have your heart, lungs, throat, important glands such as thyroid, pineal, pituitary, hypothalamus, ENT, eyes, brain, central nervous system (CNS) and peripheral nervous system (PNS) that are connected to the spine.

If you have any physical health issue related to the organs described such as BP, asthma, bronchitis, hyper/ hypothyroidism, cervical spondylitis, migraine, any psychiatric disorder, Parkinson's, Alzheimer's and many other CNS disorders, it means to say that your Chakras for this area are not functioning properly and they are either blocked or imbalanced.

Various beliefs related to bad luck, lack of love, forgiveness and genuine acceptance of self, others and situations, lack of clarity and confidence, loneliness, not knowing or acknowledging one's higher self, inflated ego, difficulty in understanding surrender, confusion about religious and spiritual texts, lectures and their interpretations, distrust in self and others, excessive prayers or chanting without knowing its purpose, fear of God, belief that God punishes, discontentment in everything and so on block and imbalance these Chakras.

Bringing your focus to every Chakra, moving your breath with strong intent and complete awareness, up and down within every Chakra and meditation on these Chakras would certainly help you unblock and balance these Chakras.

Introduce this Yogic way of living in every moment of your life and help yourself reclaim the heritage of divinity both within and around you.

Sincere seekers of material and spiritual wealth have never been deceived and have managed to reach their goal by following this Yogic principle alone.

ABOUT THE AUTHOR

Gaurav Dhamejaa, BE (Mechanical) is a well-known personality in the fields of Belief Therapy, Chakra Healing and Holistic Remedies. He is appreciated for educating, motivating and healing people by using simple techniques as a Life Coach.

Gaurav Ji (as people call him) initiated the association of Chakras with Astrology and Vastu and provided relief to his clients worldwide with the use of his relevant remedies.

He has been studying, practising and teaching holistic healing sciences for more than twelve years. In the year 2000, he did his Mechanical Engineering at Pune University and later joined his parental business of Metal Alloys. But a deep inner calling brought his attention to the metaphysical aspect of human living. He was trained by world-renowned healers and educators (from both India and the United States) in a variety of disciplines such as Astrology, Reiki, Kriya Yoga, Past Life Regression Therapy, Integrated Clinical Hypnotherapy, Astral Projection, Vastu and Rudraksha Ratna Science Therapy.

Gaurav Ji's work is inspired by his own experience of recovering from various emotional blockages during his childhood with regard to his belief system. He often mentions a chronic issue of silent emotions, which, in his perception, most people are suffering from. Through extensive study and research, continual self-experimentation and formal training in holistic healing, Gaurav Ji recovered from this debilitating condition. Soon, he started sharing what he had learned with others through his television shows, seminars and private practice. His prime approach is to make his clients aware of what they are feeling at their emotional level. He truly believes that "awareness is the first step to resolution".

Gaurav Ji lives in Gurgaon, India, with his wife and two sons.

He has propounded a Spiritual Support System that would enable his clients to indulge in self-healing for dealing with various issues.

SPIRITUAL SUPPORT SYSTEM

Most people believe that resolutions are outside themselves. This means that the external world is the source of resolution for their issues and desires. They think in this way, because they also have a belief that the outside world is the source of their problems! They feel unhappy, unsuccessful, unsupported and dissatisfied and hold others responsible for the same. Most of them blame destiny, stars and their surroundings. That is why people run after astrologers, Vastu people, palmists and numerologists to know who is causing them problems and how they can pacify everybody to improve their life.

As our senses are directed outwards, we tend to feel that everything is only outside. But the real source is inside us. We are completely ignorant that the seeds that invite troubles as well as resolutions are within us.

Successful personalities in any field acknowledge the presence of a subtle power within themselves that guides, protects and supports them. They have felt the presence of a grace that has worked in their favour to make them achieve what they wanted to achieve. That is their real secret! I call that power a spiritual power with which we all are blessed.

Spiritual Support System is the most practical "empowerment-based self-healing program" that is used for the resolution of various issues and desires. They are as follows:

Anxiety	Disputes
Lethargy/Fatigue	Obstructions
Emotional Instability	Challenges
Blood Pressure	Business Growth
Blood Sugar	Addictions
Memory Power	Low Self-Confidence
Financial Instability	Luck
Career Growth	Love
Powerlessness	Attraction
Protection	Sleep Problems
Fears and Phobias	Non-Acceptance
Body Pains	Forgiveness

And many more...

Spiritual Support System helps us activate the power within us that can heal any physical and emotional issue, fulfil any rational desire and make us experience a healthy, wealthy, joyful, meaningful and happy life. It is an organized approach to healing with four simple, easy and most effective steps:

- Body empowerment
- Mind empowerment
- Chakra empowerment
- Aura empowerment

Spiritual Support System involves healing programme and empowerment kits. For more details, log on to www.gauravdhamejaa.com